Feathers in the Wind

by

Elizabeth Martina Bishop

ONE:
One Way of Longing

Summer

Lord, the great heat of summer collapses.
A long time ago,
When the mad fandango
Of malingering shadow slid beneath sundials,
Love failed.
Loosen the wind from your hair.

Not in your lying down, nor your standing
Among your Standing Rock Elders,
Not among roundhouses in Kentucky,
Not among Shaker brethren in Dublin,
When Mother Anne loosened the wind of Holy Spirit,

Petroglyphs bloomed bright pear-shaped necklaces in untilled fields.
Apricots, marigolds, goldenrod appear as first fruits that will not last.
Matter echoes in blessed ways.
Mother Anne, if only you would give me
Two more days before I am evicted from the body.

If dervishes were beggars, don't you see, ordinary birds
Might preach to the derelict dialects of the previously converted.
Aboard the freedom train, don't you see it? Caliban is foreign.
Stay with me throughout this poem, stay with me.

Two more days, Mister Theosophist, Mr. Chilblain,
My Lumbago; then *hasta luego*.
Now set out the sideboard table for wine.
Now is the time for surgeons, Singing of ordinary joy

I haven't had so much of that, you see.
Stay with me throughout this poem at least, stay with me.
Don't abandon me.
Know that nectar will thicken on the tongue of longing.
My mother can't breathe, my father can't sing anymore.

If you have no house, be homeless; let the roof be an orphan.
Let the bee keeper of broken windows be the bar tender,
Urge nothing towards perfection.

Let it be known, all the mourning doves
Have gone directly into the vapors still singing.
I promise nothing else is happening in this poem.

Alone, a person remains anonymous as bread.
Do I know that person awakening at midnight,
Reading, writing long letters against the backdrop of blazing stars?

Constellation

What happens to the infinite when it talks back in the night?
Where I play cards, I swim like an otter in the thunder of rivers
Sown inside the embryo of rational thought.
I never asked anyone else what happens when you wake up.
Who are you and who am I to speak, to topple kingdoms in the sand?

Do we carry the list from one life to another?
Who insists on the insolence of clouds?
What happens next is unknown.
I wear old shoes to the oldest of old fairs.
There are fables about departures and arrivals.
Because Mother Earth is doing all the talking,
All of the time, some of us can say nothing.

When it rains, someone is counting out every piece of gold
And turning pockets inside out.
What truth do we know that ever existed on earth?

When your neighbor lets out her untutored moor hens
To run riot in the desert,
Like dry leaves rusting in the fire of an open wound,
Who opens the womb of the world?

I am afraid to tell Moses or Abraham what I've seen.
As a thousand wing beats circumvent the crematorium,
Accompanied by two ravens, a dove, and an owl,
I come back to myself, just in time to drink wine.
The blue silence leads us to a whirling memory
Made of light. And now I will tell you everything about myself.
Here is my passport.

It has been said these Chrichuchrua sheep have no lives,
And have lived already seven as best could.
Among the fallen sashes of wheat, will it make any difference?
I spoke of the terror of lightning,
Of trust. In Dehra Dun, how brazen the brass begging bowls.

While constellations burn in pirouettes of ash,
Nothing is resolved between us.
I cannot contend against the power of love.
I have ten minutes to complete the incompleted lines of this poem.

Nothing can be stated with any finality about my family.
Great sashes of wheat unravel in crusts of the field.
I am offering up an endless procession of totems.

It seems this generation isn't sympathetic to the polished dance
Of pollen eyes hammered in stone turquoise.
In the drunkenness of love, in the way I read this poem
Anything seems possible, and yet the sad rage of the sea
Dips my eyes in salt. Later I fled from the insane corner.

Shoes

Kneel-down-bread is the last thing you expect
To be sold from the back of a pick-up.
If you hear an unseen chorus of thrushes
Singing from a barrack,
Don't let on. Instead yawn. Detour with the pen. Read palms.
Only now can I begin to reveal
I have no dreaming left in me.
That auctioneer's gavel knocks against the table
If just a fact of life.

Stay with me, hear me, my friend.
Two safety pins hold my skirt.
Three hair pins hold up the downpour of hair.
I am not afraid. At times, street vendors
Don't need any locks on their wares.

When you feel the flames licking your heels,
Feign stupidity. For God's sake, don't say,
I have missed you
Or anything so transparent.
Remain humble. Swallow phlegm.
Act shattered as if you have just traded
A cheap edition of the blues
For an extraordinary coughing fit.
Aphorisms will move oceans.

Lovers take delight in staying up all night.
Be wise; choose the bottom of a well.
Permit a flying fish to fly.
Preserve.

The Departure
(The Ur-pflanze)
Of the Blankest Bird Colonies
Ever Known

I hear the voice of a woman telling me this. She's telling me
now she's been packing up everything for centuries. She can even let
go of the bird baths and the bird cages. Of late, she has been overly
concerned with the number of neighbors telling her they have Aides
even though they said, or what she said she said. What's the
difference? The short fall of the dollar is truly incredible to the point
anyone can believe the caravan is going. There is a distinctive blue
color of the sky. The atlas of the sky keeps changing. Somehow, I've
never seen it quite like this. I've never seen before. I don't know why
those birds died when we were gone. I found the feathers in the
living room, what more do you want to know? What more of
waltzing is not waltzing? What more of praying is no longer praying?
What more of dreams no more dreaming? What about the laundry I
was folding? I haven't swept the porch in months. Is that what you
were saying I was meant to do? Did I achieve meritorious vision in
the House of Song?

I'm already dead I said. I didn't know I was between two
worlds, betwixt and between in the land of the living. The dead
themselves, do you think they know they are dead? And if you were
fully alive, would you know of that as well? When someone dies,
their force field does not go away so easily, does it? Do their bones
pray or do I need to say it? Do I need to say this, that folding and
unfolding, unsmiling, I have been watching the dreams, those
dreams I should have been having, but I never had. I've never had
metaphors as visitors before. I've had nothing. Only I had the purity
of silence. And that is how it was. And that is how it is. Shut down.
Been there and already shut down.

Did you even ask me why I entered that Scottie in the dog show? Clipped his ears? Cleaned between his toes? Did I tell you how she burned when he didn't come in first? How she had an imagination concerning him that was quite odd. Did I tell you? I no longer dream. It's like that, is it? Is it? I mean isn't it really just that? Signs have been produced and portents among the elect that are not correct. Through this wizardry, you are not allowed to ask which element you are worshiping. You are not allowed to say stone talks back. You are not allowed to say a window burns for deceiving her neighbors. In fact you are to keep silent. Step back. But I want to know whose soul is doing the talking. She is so laid back. I cannot understand all of the words. Remember I am deaf. I live by the sea and I watch the ocean comb back the waves. I am the waves. I am the salt. It is only a short while I'll be in this body, but just long enough to say, "Hello, How do you do?" And how do I know? I know full well you are going.

She's been pulling the blinds down in her house. She's been moving from room to room. She's been sleeping everywhere on the ground as if earth were the floor she'd known from the first. She has been telling the same story year round. How Beethoven was not mad, how he did not divorce his nephew, how he was never deafened by the sound of doves, and ravens, and blue jays, and the rest of the birds surrounding his harpsichord playing. She's been moving around all the time this poor lady. How she has got a way of saying what she means is a bit of a mystery to me. Is it to you?

It had better be.

When I awoke on the poop deck, the story had completely changed. Now there was this old man telling me he had parked his wings outside the door. He said he had come to settle up a score. "Was not Beethoven here until he drowned?" he said. He talked about balancing a budget. The ledger was all messed up, he said. How when these ladies get together, there is no sense in predicting anything or telling anyone how things will go. The weather keeps on changing. No one knows who's in control. Then she asks Bill. She asks "Who is going fishing with you, Bill. Is it me or Jane today?" Then she looks suddenly away, her eyes well up with tears.

She keeps saying the next day he will drown all over again and vanish from her mind. And yet, he never does. That way she cheats the domain of death. She wants to know if all widows are like this. If every one of them fell through the windshield and then smiled when they were found sitting upside down and saying: I'm perfectly fine and in my right mind. Are you?

Laughter Having Absolutely No Reason, Simply Is

Laughter having absolutely no reason as to origin in time or place,
Goes about igniting multiple prayers from Greece, from Rome,
In silent places where the wild has willingly been named.
Yet in nameless names she has yet never had time to complete in any way.

In any case, this is how it is;
It's time to begin in the here and now, at least.
Grandmother Bird explained, it's as if a knife were cutting
Into the yellow eye of an acre of archer-colored noise before it lands
Somewhere up in the heavens.

It's like the mind of a loon anointing rooms of death
Before the loon hits water,
He drifts from the circumference of the world.
Say this does and does not matter.
Say that rooms of rain anchored here
Have never been conveyed nor rehearsed
In speech-matter steadying itself.

Say that these unwanted guests whose secrets are containing visions
That have nothing to do with what humans think of them or do not think.
The ferret wants proof of how the world works and ends in flesh.
For some souls it is easy. In dreams, they remain unmet in harems.

As soon as they are bourn, they fall asleep in the way of parting,
In the way of ghosts that have never been met in any meeting
I can think of. And now, in the distance,
If I hear the sound of some sweet birds singing
Among the pale nectar of star calyxes.
Still paler, I scarcely know what to expect.

With no thought of ever having even existed among numberless trees
Surrounding the road to the second house on the right,

Have you considered the heron is so willing to be a long limbed bird
That he prays for forty days and forty nights?

All he ever wanted was a dowry consisting of seventeen sheep
And funeral urns containing onyx, jade, chalcedony,
And juniper and evergreen-scented ashes.
Does he have any idea of how the world goes on after his death?

Of how the borrowed body of the world always had gone without him
In the dark leaves of this poem, anything is possible...
In the fist of curling muscle, Paradox of sinew, tendon, and gristle
multiply Continuing the beginning of and ending of all things.

Neither bidden unbidden will a camel emerge from a thimble
Or from a flute made of glass.
Who has ever had a sense of himself, when the infinite mind of light
Is all that reflects endlessly in the hive of light?
How many marvelous threads of light are there spinning out
From the mind of water?

It is water always I must speak enough.
On a lovely field peopled with grass
There are not enough parables of water to illuminate a cloud
After the merganser duck is gone, and the one-eyed loon
Knowing only a little of what to do
About the weeping edges of promontory.

Of those things which he has failed to do in his life–
The nature of what defines him.
Who will perfect the name of the otter breaking bread
With the darkness of arabesque, a holy shadow?

The Way

In the way of an amulet of refracted light
Bursting wide open the eye sockets, the rib cage of a zealot,
Cannot be subtracted from the body.
Her body moves forward for an instant as she crouches,
Then the jaguar is silent;
As if an unnamed witness to the room of sound in dress rehearsal.
Oh that someone might drill a tiny hole in his third eye
To put the butcher out of his misery.

For ever since he's been cutting meat,
The same thing happens over and over
As if meat were a deck of cards that needed to be cut again and again
What is the name of the indwelling spirit
Who will permit what happens to take place,
That permits the splitting of the fontanel
To sprout uneasy Tibetan tendrils?

What if the love between two friends
Were broken in that same manner,
As if brain to brain,
Unloving was then not the most natural thing in the world?
In the same way are oleanders; embroidered tombs
Of prisoner saints in suits of ivory color
Without delay attendant upon the death of roses.
Who has clay feet? Does the mud turtle?

What dances down the mind of wrens?
When I look carefully, I can see almost nothing.
I have no sense of what I did or did not say, of who I am.
Composed of little more than two drops of blood,
What is the name of the wren that bled this verse,
This jade vase that summoned alphabets back into the world?

With rabbinical line breaks that do not matter to invented grammar,
As waves shatter turquoise vases on a map of an inward shore,
What if it were or were not a case of mistaken identity
Residing in the animal brain, of an alligator in Egypt
Or the Pensacola coast?

What about the craters of the hippocampus?
How it's mind acts like a disappointed lover in crawfish country,
In the leopard choirs of souls preferring the enclosure of the soul
To meteoric forms, encompassing the silence of embrace.

Eclipsed in the moon-drenched night of the soul whose clouds
Are ever swollen with the light of dervishes.
The raw shape of haggard clouds contain no laughter,
No commentary on dream shapes.

And yet frogs, chickens, bears, skunks, and beavers all follow
The choreography, the trajectory of the gleaming river's eyeless eyes?
A bird appears untamed upon a branch.
Is there nothing to praise or extol here?
Nor even in his wildest imaginings was it ever recorded or chronicled.

The way in which, how did it happen,
Love burst through an empty cave
Where it said by seers no singing,
Nothing was ever heard in any shape or form?
Delayed on an anchor of water, it is said by prophets of the moon,
Frogs will not stop stammering, nor beavers dancing.

While rain already falling on roof and floor eclipses,
Lakes, roots, avalanches, threads, Villages' prayer soaked in wine.
How is it a faithful servant remembers his trade,
When he was the one who never practiced it?
While among branches of mimosa and eucalyptus,

The bones of disembodied spirits draw down the archer's bow.
Stammering from the throbbing tomb of lotus blooms,
The mind shatters all assumptions
About anything having to do with angels.

TWO:
Portraits

Priests in Maine

We spoke of fishermen-seers in Maine
Who turn themselves into rabbits, hares, sparrows,
Ducklings, goslings and then drag themselves
Back into men of Greece, whose souls are shaped
By the thumbprint of the moon. Unashamed, the shaman-men
Are not afraid to state they have been forever shaped
By the womb of rivers; slumped on a log like errant beavers.
The beaver people, the Canadians want to move him on,
But they cannot. Writing your name on the back of his hand,
Without even looking into the blush of mirror, they see roses
On display set at various times on the lifelines of your palm.
Who is it that shines a mirror into the waking totemic riddles
Of pine needles before lot's wife is turned into a pillar of salt?
Until the sun joins him in his astrology, singing to him,
So many Bhajans burn through the ring of fire; the fear of fear
Sung over and over again against the sting of desire.

Upstate New York: Neighbor

My neighbor tells me she has rabies like the cat.
If there were only a pill she could take,
She could correct her soul life's mistake.
It keeps coming up and the mildew grows
Antique mushrooms in the house.
The hospital released me on the condition I would give the
Dogs away and have the cats put down.
That the tablets she has brings lightning through her leg
So she cannot walk, but only with a walker.
And her dog is named Scary And she says:
"So what are you going to do?
If the doctor hadn't given me the shot
That went the wrong way round, I'd be walking now.
So what are we going to do?
Our insurance Is messed up.
If we had sued that kid that ran us through with the pick-up,
We'd be sitting pretty now. We 'd have a swimming pool, the lot.
As it is, my husband is on disability for one more week
Before he takes the air conditioning degree.
My husband is going for a master mechanic
And I'm sick of kicking around here.
And we have another dog named Timber
And a cat named Squealer,
He's a Manx, so what are you going to do?
If it keeps on going like this, I could end up in a wheelchair,
So what are you going to do?"

White Shell Woman

Why has earth broken her teeth on my soul?
Barley-blackened, sun-scorched, frozen in spring,
Reaping, she sows a harvest of souls not yet entirely known as hers.
Who is it that witnesses this myth not unlike that of Sisyphus?
White Shell Woman combing back.
The moon from moaning mask, the mask so willingly pared back
From the rind of amber moon, if she is kind enough to notice.

The task is too soon abandoned?
How will she tell my story when I awaken alone?
Moving through my waking and my sleeping,
In the steadfast gait of those who need to know.
They do not need to know facts about sonnets, linnets, and farms.
Why do I feel the sudden warmth of her heart
Shattering me almost in an instant?
What is this wing that almost carries me into exile from myself?

How can I convince her that it is torture living off the rez?
For other people, it may not be the same.
Although, I suspect them too, it well may be the same.
Before this pilgrimage to hermitage of childhood,
There is no turning back, no backward look.
Before awakening, if willingly I surrender my sari,
The legendary garment worn by women in India,
Will I glimpse Changing Woman spiraling off into liquid night?
Whirling in a myriad of stars for miles around,
Will her great belled skirt still blossom beneath
The belly of wayward stars?

Under the thick awning of meadow morning,
The width of her shadow before the dawn appears to draw me down,
In the little challenges that will not let me go
Out of the chill numbness of the dream.
Quickening, she bends, opens her dress,

A kindred spirit, breathing life into all things.
White Shell walking on red ground,
She will continue to stymie me for yet another century.

Herself as a Flower:
A Portrait of a Woman's Reflection

A woman dreamt herself into a flower.
Moving her heart into the pictures spiraling into silken threads along
the crimped edge of her crimson dress, blossoming at the breast.
Each furrow held her interest. Confessing the narrow milk of a chaste
bride, an inner rose arrowing outwardly.

Skyward, a shattered rose drew her earthward, dimly knelled the
winter of her sleep. Knotting and untying the greening vines,
unloosing the belled arc of her skirt. Scented were those briars
blowing back against the limbs, bell-tolled in psalms, unwinding as
they did in wild abandon, the fluted fire.

The rooted stem, the knotted wire of wilderness; dancing into
firmament of hymn, shamelessly she swore at clouds, thickening into
briars, half-remembered storms that were they not the ghosts of
goodness, and of god. Singing as she was, how could she not live?
Interwoven those gold-embossed embroideries from heaven,
perfumed, pollen-powdered. She appeared an envied creature.
Almost diva-drowsy seemingly, in love with love, scribing a scroll of
ancient leaves, harvested, river-fed.

Dimming the ancient mirror of herself, wrapping her thoughts in
thorns she knew what love provided. Ever so slightly ensnaring her, a
creature scalded by dreams she knew she lived, Following a swarm of
ravens kindling love if they were limber as the sparks of wind,
luminous and kind, wind that blew beyond the furled petals of her
mind.

Storm-tossed. These were the universal sparks of her own making.
Luminous were the stems of fluted fire. Of her own imaginary being,
the children flying from her body's apron of stems held her ransomed
to the sun. A woman dreamt herself into a flower. In wild abandon
this vision she embraces of herself embroidering golden skeins within
the heartbeat of Creation's Amen.

The Inner Reflection
of Mirrors

I will get even with you, my soul, deliberate friend.
Endless conversations held with you as audience will end regardless.
Unexpectedly, a perfect marksman' bow will bow;
Will prompt us from the fold, will tithe us to a tee, will enslave us,
And will barter bread for gold.
Suddenly removed form gainful employment,
Receiving stolen goods, pawning pawn eternally,
We are as we are: truly at liberty.
Momentarily, we live as we live.
From an uneven cup we draw maggots from a jar.
Drawing splinters from wellwater.
Lovingly we bless the scent of roses.
Insofar as we let life become all merciful,
Holy Water will dribble from our lips differently.
Remembering darkness and the light, we will caress raw embers.
As to the matter of this bliss burning holes in golden cloth,
My children's children, they will have to educate themselves,
As to trajectories of the mind and how it sings of bliss.
To hit the high notes among other things, these prayers,
Moving effortlessly in a soulful direction,
They will come to know how to mark with diamonds fearlessly.
Crafted, sculpted clearly in dimensions of cut glass.
Polishing weather,
How sharp the jeweled edge of the skater, the rudder,
The inner arc of the dance played back joyfully.
The inner pirouette.

The Vietnam Veteran: A Reflection

There is a man who senses the pure blue flame of oxygen in the air. In everything he does that's sacrosanct, he senses it. He senses it in the four elements in the air. He senses it and mentions that it is. And that it is in the four sacred directions and in the four sacred mountains. And so it is. Everything he says is true because he is a veteran of small winds and big winds aAnd the little rains. And he doesn't like to show how much he knows because he is a hermit and he's clear on that.

Because he is a teacher of the roads, and sometimes he explains how the states of Arizona and New Mexico were born, and how they changed the disputed boundaries to suit a cautionary tale of birth. There is no limit to his boundless knowledge about the weather and the land. He comments that the ravens have crash landed in the parking lot. It's as if a moon crater were there and it was war, he says, To watch them wrestle. Whatever's left lying there in the open spaces, people need to be informed as to what happens to whatever they have discarded. You cannot lose your mind like you can your purse in rubble.

For example, I know a woman who was going to travel in different countries of the world like Greece, and Italy, and Spain as a proper tour of duty, or something like it. And anyway she was taking her culture around about to different places including the grinding stone and the loom. And some people are against it, but she wanted others to know about the deal with the Navaho. Like as if she were on the good red road except that it seemed foreign soil, if you know what I mean. Now her husband got so jealous, he dumped her passport in the trash and swore up and down his nephews and his nieces would take his side against her. Except her sister took her side and knocked him flat upon the ground. The discussion was over. Though he swore up and down, this is how it was. And she swore up and down that it would. And still he said to all intents and purposes, he was definite about the fact. That's how it was, that the marriage would not last and she was that intent on going.

And yet she sent away for another bit of paper, and a form. And a hundred year old woman swore she'd seen her born just so she could get her baptismal straightened out, And everybody was informed that she would go and so she did. Life is like that. Nothing evil can get in the way of what should happen. Just like my great grand-daddy always said, and now he was a veteran of foreign wars and he was never wrong. No, he was not. And he grew corn higher than the sky in places where sand had turned to chalk in the blessing of the Holy Ones who are our friends.

The way I see the situation is with the heart of my breath, believing life could be different. Like in the way of knowing if a fruit tree were blooming, later it might give fruit and that tree would be a doctor to the soul and to the blessed heart of Jesus. If only people knew it; then that's all there is to say.

Give fruit, now every single pear should be canned, or at least turned around and taken so nothing is left for someone else to pawn. And don't you know I left my grandfather's wristwatch to be fixed, and didn't the man tell me to this day he hadn't a clue where he placed it and he's hiding the truth from me, an old man whom he couldn't care less about. And about dead pawn, that is precisely what I mean; it gets taken by the traders under the big tent.

Big Fairs in Chicago

At the big fairs in Chicago, the place where the cops should arrest whoever did it; but there's too many in it to know who did the smuggling. Too many middle men and too many stockbrokers. I mean you've got to be joking if you think a life would be taken over the meanest of them that's in it. It's like a world's fair for dead people but I cannot mention them by name. It's likely to bring bad luck and pull it down on their heads, know what I mean to tell you? Yes, Life is a precious gift and you cannot bathe in the air and not think God knows about the way you interfere.

Just look at the blur flame of oxygen And know that it is you. And are you doing right by me, daughter, in hearing what I have to say?

Have you got the words right for the play? My mind plays little tricks on me. Sometimes but every day I go shopping for five bags of potatoes for my breakfast, lunch, and dinner. And that is the end of my story. That is all I have to say. You'll know when the play is done for good when my footsteps are no longer seen on the side of the road that day.

THREE:
Animal Husbandry

Prosevkomai (Prayer)

Old Grandmother Bird, what has she to tell me? Is she the first one who taught me to fly? Scissor-clipped, snipped by the grace notes of a keening wind, have you ever heard her singing, lingering over Canadian territories containing a dark penumbra of compassion? What if, when I saw her, I told her I knew her? That *Joseph split the face of God and flew.*

What if she told me in one sitting, the light of all ancestral spirits were eclipsed in a single photograph, encompassing the whole world of love. And having said that, she noted among a hundred tethered threads half sewn, half embroidered, half sewn in over lapping leaf tapestries, her wedding picture fell into a prayerful *vibutti* ash.

What if she told me of a winged consort, a lioness, was guarding a tomb in Gujurat? What if she mentioned small chinks of light had gone up against the dark mouth of the moon, dropping before a small, crimson cloak? If for a moment, this be undreamt the dream in which Pyramus was killed, would she have been left standing, weeping openly?

Beneath a mulberry tree, taking the brunt of death, softening the sharpened edges, of leaves whose finite petals blushed with an infinite calligraphy of breath. Upon hearing the wind blow, would she be slain in spirit? It becomes unclear at this point in the story whether she was laughing with longing or weeping?

What was her reaction to the voice half-whispered to her body's ghost? Anasi, certainly this is not me walking beside you. This is an ear of corn, red corn, yellow corn, white corn, growing in the door jam, out leaping the scroll where the sacred chicken is killed in Senegal. Would she have said when the eyes of an ox are covered? Circling, he will go around?

Turning a mill wheel effortlessly so are man's eyes heavy-lidded, almost closed off indefinitely. Stilling the waters, calming a storm, even the deranged could save us a lot of trouble. When the rose whispered to the cypress, what was said exactly? There are simple reasons why the hawk refuses to open up the symmetry of his wings completely

Hasn't Spirit divined within us that mysterious force we do not understand, all that is? How deafening the music of angels! How does a prophet make mention of attachment, then turning around, pauses to heap praises on demons? Does the art of dowsing exist only as a way of ill-defining the sound of an unstruck bell, of straightening the vertebrae of a hunchback?

What if the toungeless silence of a solitary hermit were spent in idolatry? If a man is like a tree, so is a woman whose body, whose arms, burn with tree branches sprouting arbutus. Who admonishes a humbled spirit whose life is spent swimming up hill, Sisyphus? Meanwhile, "what a fine canoe", Blue Jay says, "I've never seen one so ornamented."

If a surgeon's heart beats wildly, running from him as on raised in the forest, blinded in the light by those who know the veiling an unveiling, what is blessed remains an uncreated blessing in scented stones within the nameless forces of creation. I listen. A woman is speaking unspeakable wisdom. The woman's body opens like a flower.

Do you know her? What if, in the end, all things known by spirits were to depart? Emanating from the plant body, nestled in the teachings of the Mother of all Sorrows? If palaces unlocked their leafy doors only for the purpose of measuring thirty cubits,would we feel the call of God and the journey changing the traveling?

Possessed by the divine intoxication of beating heart, in a golden vessel drumming in two worlds, when one garment is cast off, the other taken on: she tells me she really has little idea of what occurred. I will tell you again my half-story of sowing and reaping into which Joseph's body vanished. And yet, without warning, in the middle of everything, fully he grew into a inner knowing.

What was he reaching for? A rafter of smoke? A reed? A water jar?
A nectar cave? Japheth boarding an ark? A mud turtle, one with
terrible claws, scribbling adobe villages in mud? The name of the
mountain, Mauna Kea, yet, as soon as the floodwaters water subsided,
it was clear Mother Earth was flattened beyond recognition.

Her body, A Canoe-like-a-Chief's-House had been created. Coconut
milk, offerings of pig entrails were given over. Half-completed the
quilt story, she almost tells. Heart scalded, the speech,the mind of
memory. The quilt untilts its thimbles and unravels death-defying
leaps, out leaping lightening.

In a dream of natal return, she does not recount a story about swans
idling in a green willowed sanctuary of fern-lined rivers. What if she
revealed the guardian gate-keeper, drowning in God? What if she, the
wandering pilgrim, fell into endless labyrinth of curlicues where
hummers were buried beneath the rooted mysteries? In the upper
worlds, it is said water always runs past the grape vines until reaching
Father Sky,

At that time, a young girl is placed in a hollowed out canoe. No one
asks her where she's from.

On no account should she leave. Until the moment the vessel touches
land, she does not speak

When the canoe touches earth, seeking rest, diving, she swims within
a hairbreadth of the mountain. The magic wand of water impregnates
her/ later, she gives birth to a daughter.

Grandmother, is that the way it has always been?
This my first time hearing this story.

Yes, my daughter, that is the way it has always been.
The wise ones knew of the flood that was coming.

Whose words, these contrary iridescent jewels spoken from within
timeline parallels? Seeing the wine outpoured on the ground, I heard
her say: *As a guest of a fearful inn-keeper, almost silenced, I wanted to be the*

split star-seed-kernel of an almond tree. What is this sense you have of yourself, nothing? I have no sense of existence. I cannot Taste my own essence.

Such was the cause of my coming to this part of the world.
With the whole length of my body, without drowning, how can I meet the one who lives within?

Why do you go on sleeping, while, in truth, water rises and the bowsprit horizon splits the landscape? If I were the one caught up in the shuddered house, if it caught fire, would you get out? Without the pick of luck, would you tangle in the wake of little words burning?

What if the manuscript of weather were contagious? Would you admit a sorceress lived in this place? What swims through walls? A long time ago, were you born without a caul?

Why do you persist in running away from you body's remarkable good fortune? Was it true you were thirsty? What rendered your life ordinary, commonplace as breath?

Did you welcome difficulty? Everyone walks alone. Mother Earth follows the sun. Nobody pulls anyone else along. People are only talking about entering, or belonging. Coming and going, they never have departed from the soul's circumference. Unmet, hadn't they partaken of suffering? When can we tear down the stage set?

And, what if it were true, (I get the firm sense of this from the shape of your letter), down wind of where we were, there was nothing but praiseworthy, blameless shrines? I'm not one who falls under the sway of another. Cast your bread upon the water. If the soul cannot find you, you can find ways to shelter under a blind, soft turning wind.

In the fullness of hunger, what does it matter, famine soothes the body with a warm emptiness.

If chosen to have you rib cage split open by knowledge, what does it matter? If, in the sorrow of having been born, nothing owed, nothing was owned, no loss. Or, were you so dazzled by the moonlight, you made a drunkard out of karma's desire for balance?

Could you have lingered in the open spaces of the photograph forever? Weathered the ashes; weather the bones of the body, transfiguring light into transcendence.

What if there was absolutely no point to being a photographer, an architect of weights and measures; of dandelions, roses, lilacs, marigolds? I'm told divine inebriation has no form, no formula.

What if that photograph taken by the photographer existed solely to maintain the proper flow of energy? What multiplies the garden of delight? Without apology, who reads your heart?

Without a magnifying glass, nothing stands for anything, yet half-doctored surrender is half sensed, half-felt. Everyone living in the same place has imagined the first tint, the blush of death without regret.

Why not touch up the photograph and lighten everyone's hair?
But, here is where the lovely music of the harpsichord abruptly ends.
Neither do we have any idea where the picture is leading us,
just like the others, gathering up the threads, I dreamt of letting go.

Herons Emerging
from Ikebana

Poured into the shape of water, Monster Slayer and the Twins,
Mother Earth will allow for only one teaspoon of compassion.
If more than on vapor sings aloud from the cave,
Tongue tied and absurd, remember to conserve water.
Sprinkle you bed sheet sprinkled with rose geranium water.
So what if the flesh is withered in the way of wrinkled skunk.
Cabbage saw leaf palmetto, or rosemary, or tansy curlpepper plant,
Trust me; you definitely need a new doctor, Mark ides hailing,
This time from the Hebrides instead of that port town in Cyprus.

Trust me, I'm working hard at trying to create
A new body-building technique,
Yet, mostly I've been edited out of the tourist brochures.
Ram left his kingdom of the deaf, dumb, and blind people,
For the people's democracy.
I found I was barely able to accept, he was well able to protect
My brother and myself from bandits. The power of thought
Equals half a gram of marigold milk sprinkled with rosemary leaves.
Later, when I sold his tattered coat to the king of Armenia
For a few dollars, people came back to me and said
I made a poor real estate deal.

And when the man met me he asked me straight away,
"Where did you say you dog came from? Where was it, Chicago?"
Its two o'clock in the morning, give over.
When appropriate, demand professional help.
Where did you hear it said, the almanac from El Dorado is written
In invisible ink, stamped with the tattoo of a White Man's foot?
From the corncrake, the linnet, and the cross-eyed mole,
You may compete the teaching. What the man from Black Hat
Has to say may not be to your liking.
At a time like this, you may need a compass
To reach the edge of the Mogollon Rim.
Wind currents have always confused the mystics.

Tumble into bed with the blind wisdom of the ancients.
Review anthills and cornrows. Book knowledge will fill you
With the emptiness of compassionate knowledge.

Everyone knows about the mortgage.
The cricketer's estate was sold out from under
The wing beat of warblers and flying thrushes.
An auctioneer's gavel will list the acreage.
Floodlights will reveal your instinct for gathering
Hand-painted furniture, rush mats, and antique kerosene lamps.

The Big Picture Defies
the Lament of the Sparrows

Were you to declare every blade of grass
A sacrament leading to a gravesite,
In Collooney, or is it Cobh,
An eaglet landing on a branch
Might seem a lightning flash,
Polishing a blank mirror made of sky.

How is a human life to be lived
That eyes may vision into canny crevices,
Might unhook palaces of air and not be bedeviled
By the dark purse of flesh?
A river's toungueless notion of light is always changing.

As nearly as a peddler sinks his boat
Into a Ganges sinkhole filled with mud,
I study the canaries in the cave
To see whether breath is part
Of the infinite stem of belonging..

A lover may not always be
A trusting friend but just
On a riderless horse for a time.
Horse whisperer, the beginning hint of logic,
For human attachment and thirst seems beguiling.

There's a firmament of indiscretion.
Sally walked out on Jerry, and Jerry walked out on Tim.
Whatsoever game was played was played as if a chorus
Of thrushes in the back room always knew the tune belonged
In an asylum of longing.

I knew a hawker who once played the Uillean pipes well.
It was a pity he died at twenty.

His brother, Sean, not long ago he was found wasted in the street.
A harpist, and a bassoonist, two years longer
And he might have made old bones.

No one was surprised when Sean quit the body,
Bowed before the veins of music, he was no more.
He fared no better than those princes of Egypt,
John Faw, for example, whose name was outlawed
From the wine-stained lips of Elizabethan players
And their coterie of ill-mannered servants.
Cursed and blessed in the same breath,
He wrecked havoc on his lineage:
"Shakespeare was mad and used to dance
On table tops," is what John Faw would say,
As he dipped his counterfeit brains
In gold and silver tender.

When a song is played perfectly for a stretch on a *bodhran*,
Does the sting of the drum hurt the ears ever so slightly?
When, scaling the clouded sky, a tern appears to temper a caress
As he steers his wings and showers certain blessings
On a whirling dervish girl, tarted up in finery
On a cobbled street. What does that signify
To a dream interpreter; to one who reads leaves?

What of the fabled girl who claims her Irish blood
Is rooted in the earls of Kinsale, the one pledging loyal oaths
To non-existent kings, from whom she swears she's descended?
Alongside a red-bearded Viking and all belonging to her,
What of her great aunt's cousin, the one with the gammy leg
And the slight crick in the back of the neck? Being well born
Is she of the gentry, if even well-turned out, ill-tutored;
With great child-bearing hips and mild dyslexia?

Once I knew of a great blue heron
That drowned on the river Cong.
The woven hair of the bird sang in a long river of Celtic dragons.
A feathered tunic could not mimic
The comic wound torn from the great surround

Of wind-stippled water.
The steeped clouds blew back against the brow of the hill into smoke.

What difference does it make? Sparrows are content
To roost into mystic cells in winter and in spring.
Perhaps Martha is the one relative. And twice removed
The woman who smoked a corn cob pipe.
Don't waste your time with keening.
Consulting diviners or idolaters is forbidden.
Life is simple. Know the newborn blades of grass
Are soaked in reunion with lovers who have endured
The almost moon-drenched longing for goodness
Is as mysterious as air.

Twice transfixed is the one who never existed,
Who is the person half pictured in history of bloodshed?
As for example, when Genghis Khan lit those cat tails
And saw what happened next when the town went up.

In the half story, in the most transitory moment,
There's always a blessing of the Trojan horse.
There's always one unknown who wasn't pictured,
And remains mysterious. Who is Sean exactly?

As wine disappears inside the wine keg
During the last part of the journey
I forget the name of whoever it was, they never left off lightning.
The corn cob pipe and drinking, the one who swigs the last drop
down?
What does it matter?
Hasn't the ocean always swallowed amulets?

Mother Spider

I

If, dangling errands of spittle mid-air,
Mother Spider were to bring forth a changeling child
In spring, how would you recall her truth?
If confessing a hairbreadth of beginnings,

Half ending in doxology of plant medicine,
She was the one to bend the tilted roof and floor of thread,
In the breadth and width of cloud still ranging with its birds,
If she were the one that in her unknowing knew,

How to bind, to bend, to withhold the wedding
Of a thousand leaf-strewn rivers in her care
Beyond underpinnings of salmon filled deltas
In raven filled shadows, across uneven weirs,

Braiding and unbraiding the moon drenched hair of willows,
How would you praise, how live in the unfolding abyss
Of a thousand petals whirling in a momentary ghost
Garment of timeless sages? In an unguarded moment,

What question would you raise? Waking, how breathe
The sleeping dream back into brother sheepherder's
Pelt that he might find unseen healing plants
Burning little circles raw beneath his wandering feet?

II

What did you see in your sleep that upon waking?
Half-hidden, painting itself in a thousand colors,
The soul became drunk on its own transformation,
You want to put food in your mouth and drown yourself.

But even inside your cave you're not ungrateful
For sun pouring its elegant garden into womb
Where a dust-ridden oasis from which you cannot recover
Doors keep opening and shutting in the presence

You felt delight at the sneering wife, at the scolding
Of linnets, a disbelieving pagan somehow you gathered
Everything could be retracted in an instant,
The eyeless weathered horse could throw the rider

Shouldered to earth a seed may outlive a feather.
Hath the rain a father?
Who will describe
The wind arising that will tear the firmament
Of fire because of love and love alone?

Water outshines past troughs of the nectar sieves
Of rivers. On small green islands, herons stand,
Steering past fragrant inlands, then another
Until each other's bird is melted stone.

Goat Auction

I

I I've sold my pallet to afford the dowry
Undreaming the riches of a thousand birds,
Unhook the ghost of surrender.
Resilient ghost, I fear the dream of embers
Will re-eat itself. He who lingers brooding in the shadow,
Soon he will become a shadow.
Whoever unpeels an onion, will pluck out
Eyeless the braille night sky of its stars,
And shed a tear the size of an unplucked chicken
Deprived for all eternity of its feathers.
The mimosa will unlock its compass of leaves.

II

I plucked the wild figs. I noted the number of frogs
Drawn down into the green pools of water.
I stopped the locust in their tracks.
A butterfly obeyed the sound of wind,
And brushed my cheek.
The wrens, unchecked, flew in rivers:
They were what I did not say about deliverance.

III

Not in the least, where the last spoken words of grieving are,
The heart gladdens as it softens,
And gathers the falling peach blossoms.
But that which cleaves to matter does not matter,
And silence matters less than the green stones, fern covered
Where otters bathe their bodies in the moon drenched river.
I can no longer untangle my hair in secret.
But as a soothsayer of words, I may be impervious.
In a rumor of still more impertinent bees, you should know this:

IV

I let the rabble of goats
Nibble on the corrugated tin roof.
Rain has fallen all night. A little bridge of raindrops arch
Over my heart,
With the blunt edge of a sharpened knife.
At night, I mark the places where my life cannot unbend
The truth. Where are the birds that first flew from heaven?
Man asks; what is the truth? What is the purpose of life?

V

I ask, what is the truth of hunger?
The silence of creation will not feed starvation.
How loud is the tongue of angels
In the silence that shapes the meaning of what is forever mute?
My children eat invisible tomatoes filled with worms.
The rotten fruit falls apart in their tiny, innocent hands.
He who loved a shadow is exiled from the light.
A thousand thimbles fall from the hem of my tattered garment.
No one is the wiser for it.

VI

How pure is the prayer of mercy
For he who loves not out of kindness, but out of misery?
Somehow, the flowers I carried in my woven basket
Made with palms that blurring the hooves of burros,
Have withered. It's not from lack of prayers,
Attendant upon my sick uncle's body,
That all this has come about. It's not from lack of love
That drops the nectared honey from the willow branch.
It is simply, whatever I purchased from the city
Did not suffice. A storm resurfaces and slides down
The back of the mountain for no reason.
Is all this because it's spring or not?

Fish

Here lies a fish. He stares at everything and nothing.
Eyeless, he lies dejected, his soul cannot look back.
As light refracts light, clearly the world looks terrified.
Swarming around him, surrounding him like mosquitoes
A school of silver minnows genuflecting, startle
Without warning. Lugging the body's air, martyred he dies.
Discomfited by love, by the refusal of decent hooks.

To bear the gifts of nourishment and food,
In the way he looks, he paves a road to injustice.
At the ebb and flow of salt-filled waves,
The man's boat is heaved upon shore.
Filled with sadness that he cannot control,
Glaring at the ocean's moon-filled ocean roaring
At morning, in a wicker satchel, he carries it.
Bearing the monogrammed initials AE, he carries it.

He carries it, the man carries the fish to the mountain.
Drawn from his back pocket, the small black comb
Is by now a ritual object for shadow player of the dawn.
Unsmiling, the man combs the unspeakable lice,
From his blue, black hair, newly cut and greased.
Almost mistaking himself for someone else, the man
Steers the mirror away from his pock-marked face.

The ravens sing of purgatory.

Cougar in Winter

Catching sight of Cougar moving eastward, I sing of the winter
and the wind. Bidden or unbidden, not by anyone in any quarter,
behold the sinews of the Cougar. How unceasingly he moves!
Sightings have been reported, in fact, numerous treaties spell out the
details of what belongs to whom and exactly what that means to each
of the parties concerned. In fact, treaties go to great lengths to explain
the in's- and out's of everything about water rights, about mineral
rights, and about how the land and air should not be bought or sold.
Treaties explain about how in the past everyone's head was measured
by the Department of Interior to find out whether intelligence could
be conveyed by the yard or by the inch. Even up to the present time,
people are still interpreting the boundaries of the loon, the egret,
never mind the hidden blind mallards left out in the regions on loan
from a map of Northern country.

Let's not talk about the detours of the condors and the
whooping crane. And do you know what? I saw a great bald eagle
yesterday! Be that as it may, I do not want to exclude the Cougar
from the region of my heart. In his tribe, he is both respectable and
chaste. Clearly, his presence is not to be dickered with as his shadow
is not actually drilled in any scriptural text, or in any known or
unknown catechism; heard or unheard in no uncertain terms with any
finality by any who take note of these things in a hurry. I wonder if it
ever occurred to you that love, as we know it, is simply unavailable.
That the lonely are becoming more lonely, and Mother Earth is
responsible for none of this.

People are debating about whether they just have to look
after themselves and everything else will take care of itself, including
the stock market and the wilderness. There is a drought in America.
In Europe, there are great floods, and a woman known as Elizabeth
is building a healing center there. She claims that the center will be
on dry land next to great healing spas, where the curious will flock
and the unruly will become less rowdy.

And the details of the afterlife appear meticulous as bone and bread as the populace is disowned by history and through prophecy is being deprived of any real sense of the imagination or history. And it's anyone's guess whether what will come afterwards will be beguiling or ill-advised in the matter of the living and the dead. And do you know, when Cougar comes sweeping down the mountain, he smile. Fires flicker and die down. Out of desperation and hysteria, many divas request copies of his paw prints or copies of his furry autograph alone.

No substitutes for such replicas of authenticity on loan. These rooms of snow represent the place of Cougar can own and divide as he will. Promises are held over for yet another century. Whose destiny is shaped by Death will never be revealed. Yet, somehow we intimate quietly to ourselves in the shape of stopped breath that, about such creatures, we are woefully ignorant and doubtless; bereft of faith. Destiny takes us somehow unaware and the knowledge that snow is eternal and delectable as love, shaped in the wake of stars for the sake of the furry shoulder is sometimes not enough.

How remarkable these territories, half-charted, that define the surround of Cougar. His refection blurs the several stars he stirs in the sashay of his non-existent tail. These have nothing to do with uncommon prophecies by common troubadours. Neither are they in keeping with several of Heaven's starry histories regarding the extent to which we want to hide or to fortify those leper- filled stories brought up sharply before us before all worlds were to have been made. How is it we knew the facts about how purgatory keeps on burning in the afterlife?

Does anyone really know about the hereafter? Sikhs sit in Lebanon and debate with their bubble pipes. They are still there after all these years yearning for answers. I am kept in the dark about the way in which history was supposed to have been foretold, about how we were all supposed to have been eventually burned at the stake, deliberately and fully by this time. All of this for striking gold, that is all hearsay so I have been told. Were not love possible, none of these words would be provoked from the hidden spring in the garden. Have you been there? How do you know?

Grandfather Bird

Once, a long time ago in my soul's orchard,
Singing in the innermost branches of my dream,
Out of nowhere, a blue jay came to me.
Sighing, he was beside himself and weeping.
You know he barely could contain himself.

About the state of the world, he was uncertain.
He said the map of the world would change.
He said the purse of the rivers would dry up.
Hailstones would make craters out of the dust.
All of this would fall from a tree where he was singing
As freely as the beauty of the air that he aimed for.
He sang his forefathers had always gleaned the truth.

He said that life, as we have known it,
Was unpredictable and chill with omens.
He said that wine would spill out from hidden springs
But that nothing could save us from ourselves.
With great urgency in his voice, he repeated
He believed and felt life was as it was
He felt it was full of unstoppable occurrences,
Catastrophes, cacophony, and silence.

As he sang before me, I heard him clearly.
Faltering, trembling, his was the voice of continents repeating.
In essence what had been said a long while back
In the time of prophecy, when prophecy was an acceptable way
Of talking about the weather and the birds
And everyone accepted the truth as if a suit of clothes.
Repeated by the wren, hawk, and sparrow, father of many
Generations, the voice of the jay was a very ancient voice.
The voice of the grandfather speaking
From within the inner dimensions of the perfumed ethers,
Stemming sweetly from the voice of oneness, his voice.

Knowingly, unwittingly, that voice taken upon itself
To transmit the diverse vows of life's parallel generations
Seed brimming, spilling, blossoming, promise-filled, and filled with love.
What made you think of it before the altar? The testimony of
Plant medicine, that which returns the compliment of birth
In a season which knows not full well the extent of its harmony.
Knowing in knowing and unknowing, what is meant by prayers
recited; Ever flowing on occasions when breath breathing breath
repeated in Rounded voice within the contour of the wind.

When upon the wrist of the mountain, that voice is felt that is your
own Revelation's heart witnessing the movement of molecules
dancing, Singing, moving. When awakened by sage and juniper,
Restored as mountain wedded to mountain, shored up
With mountain snows, unwinding, sliding down, cascading, consoling,
Breathing into the wind-driven clouds, thinning,
The timelines are getting so close, so as not to be able
To remark upon it, to bridge, to forge the slanted river
At a respectable distance. The specks of consciousness
Would be an unthinkable premise by which to live.

Grown slimmer by the minute, life is brimming
With unseen promises of the wind,
Seen and unseen in penny glimpses.
It is men who are the ones who have always been
Somnambulist and sleeping.
A Suspect of flickering incandescence,
A glimmering of wings never fully theirs.
These are those rivers of men, those backstabbers,
Their habits deeply engrained, though entertaining.

The unraveling of days, hidden from them
When bidden by the scent any wrong doing.
The cadences dream ripple beside them,
The impossible wedding of land and land
Across soul continents of watery firmament.
I know what is meant by the ornament,
The slip- stitching of impossible threads
Into which the mind he plunges.

With a whispering within
Inaudible, I hear the voice asking:
Am I not yet drowning?
Am I not yet burning?
Am I yet a salve to salves?
Am I yet a prayer among prayers?
Am I yet a stone to stone transfiguring?
Circumspect and somehow daring,
Whirling within the innocence
The indifference of love.
The blue jay floats above the world
Anointed by redemption, as he is
Invisible as God.

Whose air is this I am breathing?
Heard in the voice in which he is asking
As bird still sings unequivocally of justice.
He almost asks, discerning what is allowed
In the din of the world in which he is residing.
What is permitted to be asked is absurd.

A Day for Hawks, Flagstaff, 2002

I

This is a day for hawks.
I am not I, nor you, you.
Whatever else may be said,
I say to the hawks,
You are not of the body.
This not what you see,
Is not what I am,
Is not of the ancestors spirits
Lit up in feathered incense sticks.

II

Is not of a wick held up before the heart
Offered to a hand trembler,
Is not of a weaver's seemly pattern,
Woven in one of three hundred patterns of a blanket,
Is not of a seer's infinity.
Nor of a garment, steadily woven in a trembler's hand
Convening dark against dark.
Neither the converging of threads
Ambling through a thimble nest of thorns.
Whatever else anybody might have said,
Self meeting self is more than watery vapors
Meeting the wrinkled shore.

III

More than a diver's raft
Running rough shod over rapids,
I must remind myself fully,
Not what I am, just lonely enough
For a time remaining only in ramshackle huts,
After that, rather what I meant is to say is this:
I am but an infinitesimal fragment,
A being held apart. Blase Pascal,
The heart stopped up against glass.
Vine, bone, and vein, slung shyly
Within the vine of proverb's unguessed wine,
Where no drum beats its pollen path long enough

IV

Unless that soaring god comes down,
Fearless and is in goodness felt.
Unless against a clear heaving
Cleaves sky, calm and clear at evening;
Clouds only may be what are left
Of these courteous birds. I say to the birds:

V

How many of you are left?
What may be said of moon and sun?
Swaying in fits and starts, in the wake of infinity's curve,
These wings inform the mind.
You are not what you say you are,
Nor any of the scarred crevices in the brain.
I ask the hawk:

VI

Betraying a commitment
To the self that is not self,
This compassion is invisible milk.
This, what you see, is not the body
Nor a teardrop of creation's mark.
Not a jewel, nor a crown.
All else lies within the imagination
Is but a lie.

VII

I walk across the park.
I see fountains pouring down
A host of feathered water.
The winged palaver
Of the hawk, red-tailed and quick,
While he parries for the price
Of smaller birds
To the edge of heaven.
His actions are absurd
Before the wind.

VIII

Every gesture of the rabbit,
Every motion of the fox,
Is under unique surveillance
Of a trickster coyote's camera that,
While flattening distances,
Clicking the shudder,
Stupefies the observer and the unobserved.

IX

It is not enough to bare witness.
In a meadow of questions,
Where there are no answers
I continue waking.
Whatever curved space this is,
This is not a carapace, the place of riddles,
But space occluding the bright burning;
Occurring between earth-sky, sky-roof,
Body, bird, burial, and resurrection.
All this a re-enactment of gravity,
An existential rehearsal for existence
Not yet fully aware of itself.

X

It is the kind of agreement that
Cannot be fed
By anything that's human.
Clearly let it be said:
This is a day for hawks.
Calm and clear,
The sky moves the upward ladder of its roof
I lean down to pick up a feather
That has been left for me or for another.
Awakening, opening and closing,
The very elder brother of this bird
Is the last bird to hurry on.

FOUR:
Elegies

Blackfoot Blanket

What of the ponderosa pattern of the Blackfoot blanket?
A Pendleton almost reaching to his feet, but not quite.
Who keeps repeating words to her? Can she tell who's speaking?
Is it her doctor? Is it her cousin?
A neighbor whose name she doesn't quite remember prays with her.
But she doesn't want to pray, not yet.
To this day, she is never quite sure as to the way in which it
happened. As the stilted clouds look down on her,
She wonders as to the true meaning of the word *widow*.
Someone else tells her there is a perfect time and place for everything.
Such emptiness.
She has no place to put the glut of too many pressed shirts.
The sideboard cupboard, tells her the linen closet is empty.
Loneliness, a traveler travels through the whispered skirt of water.
A woman is talking about having socks darned in the morning,
But, Joseph has departed into the night
In songs that are still sobbing with light.

Funeral for
Parachute Jumpers

Dressed up in her silk parachute jumpsuit,
Surrendering to the deafening music of swans,
What ensures deliverance of White Shell Woman?
Driven among the unsung resonance
Blurred in arabesques, wave upon wave,
Singing from her holy thighs.

What is this sweet commingling of wings
Broken upon the belled skirt of innocence?
In furious longing for the salt wings,
Drowning in rabbit brush, love's memory
Painting iridescent flames in the death-defying
Leaping of Thunder Beings.

Impermanence

Why do you think you can walk on water,
On hot embers, through walls,
When life hangs by a thread, unraveling?
If gossamer roof and floor collide,
Sliding off the world,
What holds the tent pole up?
It is only a stampede of minutes, a nest of threads,
A cupola of air.

If a spindle retracts its tethered thread,
Then wool is not wool;
The laughter of the pattern not accessible.
If a lightning flash does not occur,
The hinges of flame will not occur.
The hinges of flame will not open.
The bird falling from the burning branch,
Leaving an ocean of ash, invisible,
Unguessed, untraced, spindrift in the air.

Wings

A thousand wings
Brush past your face.
How close they came,
Those lean circumferences
Of spring, and left.

The seasons burn beneath you feet.
The heart has forgotten
How to tick.

Ants lick up all the honey
Left on earth.
It is a trick to learn
How to meditate.
A large piece of clothing
Will make you feel
Less lonely for yourself.

Words are not about breath.
Breath is about breath
Enfolding the wings of your body.
That's all.
The breaking waves
At my feet are almost deafening.
Unasked, love holds an empty cup.

FIVE:
To The Gatehouse

Unraveling

Adding to the sadness of existence,
Has the human heart no place within the planet?
Moment to moment, what difference does it make?
Traveling before the stage set of Hogan,

Who am I to think of sundering threads,
Unraveling ancestors from Coteau des Prairies?
At times, I feel pulled away, drawn down,
The focal point eclipsed by circumferences.

Knowing full well all is recited perfectly
Within the sculpted lines of the dreamtime,
Isn't it so all is made perfect, blameless,
Creating watery threads within Manitou's body?

Anchoring blindness, will an unlit candle
Burn, already drowning in darkness, its withering,
Luminous light? What if a surgeon could doctor
The wilting waves? What if, uprooted, a mountain

Could forsake the tilted lantern of cypress?
What cottonwood, what evergreen could extinguish
Its silent fire, knelling the tongue of an unstruck
Bell, like well water coursing from the ground?

The Pawnshop of Souls

It is said by the ancestors, this is the way things are done,
The way they have always been done.
We stand for the lives of other, for seven generations.
Elders have defined our footsteps, and where we are going.

It is said by the priest, the basket must be unwoven, unbraided,
Every grass blade must grow back into the earth, unsung,
The spirit unheard, the Hogan reversed in direction.

The people ask: Whose is the spirit unheard?
Is it the inner voice performed in the elder' lives,
Rehearsed but not defined? Is it the outer religion,

Defines all too clearly, affirms baptism or you'll burn in hell?
Perhaps souls have arisen in unison. In this bartering of souls,
Dead pawn, or are heaven's pockets are lined with gold?

The Recipe

A master told his student that to live on nettles
Was a sign of one who was greatly devoted to God;
Lord Krishna, Buddha, Christ, or Changing Woman.
Later, while out walking in the desert,
Under the great whirling stars,
The student caught a glimpse of a coyote eating nettles.

"What must I have been thinking?' the coyote said,
And wished he had feasted on elderberries,
The ones that grow in Naslini were so delicious."
But the student did not hear.
"Look at coyote," he thought, "so devoted to God.
Surely he is doing the right thing.
He is foraging for nettles and eating them in bunches
As if they were grapes from the finest vineyards of Napa."

Thinking to gain in ascendancy toward enlightenment,
The student began grasping at nettles,
Until his knuckles started to bleed.
Later, he put them in his begging bowl
Saying," This will make a fine meal later:
The path toward enlightenment not so very far away."

Knots

Unraveling the knotted roots of time,
I died. Diving deeper than I dared
Into the feathered arcs of clouds, unasked
The unmaking of the mask's existence.

I told myself I'd drunk too may cups
Of wine. A thousand alleluias meant
As much to Silenius carousing in painted waterfalls
As when coaxing the knife from the sheath, time asked:

Why doesn't every dervish dance?
Keeping inner and outer drowning sacrosanct,
Overturning a cup of wine outpouring
Grief form Dionysius, your body's garment.

What barber dies while a donkey's ears are snipped?
To keep from dying and undying, is the soul, horse-whipped?

Water

Without the water of the body, we could not
Live at all, nor predicate the weather of the soul.
The water you want may drown you in clairvoyance,
Refusing to make you full of wisdom, dutiful, cheerful.

Among dreadful piles of bones, plenty of ghosts
Will be introduced to you as son-in-law, mother-in-law,
Yet anyone of them you envision sitting,
Standing, walking may not revisit you.

When one day Blue Jay returns from fishing,
Half-expecting him to extinguish several
Prairie fires in the land of the living, his aunt
Asks him to obey her. Still she does not.

Instead, he makes misleading statements about
The nature of war. In the process of mistaking
A salmon-colored painting for a metaphor,
He deserves all the while a stone canoe.

The Blind

I recall how it was learning how to read the inked scrolls
in my youth, the younger generation found the truth
in everything, not necessarily the truth. I've been looking up old
friends in my address book. I've been researching the nameless
almanacs,

in codicils, in alphabets, in scripted documents explaining
how to disown truth, how to pull out teeth, how to dog-walk stray
dogs, how to pendulum and dowse for diseases, how to avoid jay-
walking, railroad manuals, handbooks, how to avoid being left-
handed,

how to avoid uprooting calendulas, and roses, how to avoid
doing the dog paddle, the butterfly stroke, how to win and lose
at backgammon and chess, and how to receive enlightenment
rereading the handbooks for paralytic, the arthritic, and the lame,

including the deaf, dumb, and blind ambulatory schools
those whose wheelchair proof indexes guiding those who prefer
to dawdle letting their legs dangle in pools near waterfalls,
in seaside places in Blackpool in the Corrib in the Yangtze,

in the veiled interstices of weather, how is it the colorblind
in the pagodas of their imagination serve burnt toast
to entrepreneurs who because they have no hands or feet
with which to gesticulate depend entirely on the antics

of the moving picture and the mosquito netting defining them.

The Physiognomy of Plants

What is it exactly Chinese gourmands are so very fond of
Rendering their lives as vulnerable as ice-borne?
Winged seeds, flown into codicils and tendrils,
Retelling them how to live their lives in Padua, entering,

Exiting among stamens, anthers, a sixteen branching plant,
Termed Goethe's palm; a cosmic physiognomy?
Luminous and flickering, little by little, their fur subsides.
Perhaps it will be announced in the morning,

The nameless wedding of opposite, paradoxes
That makes the body shake with invisible roses.
A mountain lion is a creature to be shaded by palm trees,
And trade winds until they die in Sertung and Panjang.

Whatever covered by a cloud blanket of ash
Unmasked, you soul will drown in it completely.

SIX:
Divination
for Dowsers

The Witzelsucht
(The Laughing Disease)

I

I said that I would settle in that house.
Most people have learned to sit for years before
Their lives are purified. There is no cure
For grief, she said. There is no cure for you.

The you or the not you in my life, the way
I miss a door jamb, linger unmet in doorways,
Linger in frames when I should have left,
The way I rime the ground with hoarfrost,

If you laugh, if you speak, you sink or swim
Standing motionless in the partita's unfolding.
If you dance the waltz of cupid's disease,
Who wins at poker, who wins at bridge?

II

Who untangles the synaptic branches of the brain?
What soul is in communion with numberless angels?
Could they have been in communion with ants, with larvae,
With the genius of locusts spiraling into integers mapped by
Disquistiones Arithmeticae?

When the ground swells with the marking of a grave,
Who is to blame?
Into the pit, ant lions slip blamelessly.
She promised I would have a daughter named Nadia
Shouria, We would live in Northern New Mexico.

And then we ascended the peak at Yosemite Park.
We concluded most trees grew antlers of extreme antiquity.
Two distinct creators must have been at work.
What are we to the ears of God?

Burlesque

He would have asked you the name of the one last poem you had written. But he thought better of it. Better of it since before the run off of any water He knew the edge of the river, the place where she had gone and mapped departure. In the village where we were born and died, in time the emperor grew perplexed by the timelines. And what was in them, the way the girls dyed their hair red and drifted into dreaming places. Where wine was wine no longer and yet they sang.

I have perfected this sonnet In a mindless place where among blooming chrysanthemums there is an empty place Where swallows come and go unaccompanied by the fleeting songs of old age Of late auspicious lute players and gamelon-players run from me.

Every place that ever existed was robbed of its hidden granaries and treasures. Those fleet of foot now carry arthritic limbs. The noise of birds is deafening everywhere. What was suggested as a cure for old age is an infusion of dandelion win in marked intervals. Walking slowly among catalpa-lined avenues peopled by mimosa, plum blossoms, and acacia,

I realize, bit by bit, already growing blind and having nothing really new to say, No verses I write over the course of time will turn any heads, or make any difference.

Invocation

Grandfather Bird refuses to spread out her wings,
What for? Doesn't she know the world sings as it chooses.
They're auctioning off birds from every branch, trees, clouds,
Waterfalls, a spiritual fire that needs quenching.

Talons grapple with the wind of fire.

So what is the sense of leaving your house?
Without knowing it, you're tangled in the hair of branches
Perching on a roof, or on a veranda stairway,

Beneath the intelligence of the body,
A second story, roof, floor, walls swimming:
Continuous sequences encompassing
Elemental cells, yet some deepening.

Awakening what love between friend and friend.
Unadorned god-demon selves, light-dark
Retracting laws of gravity, before birthing Logos:
Stark axial history of Lao-Tsk, Lien-Tsp.

The Ur-pflanze

Have I packed up everything? I've sold my straw pallet.
I've sold my cows, my goats, my sheep. I've been looking
For something growing along river banks. To reveal the nameless plant
Would be a sacrilege of the ordinary.

I have buried an antique fan at the foot of the mountain,
A long way away from where I live, the dead
Pass quickly when they go, a long time ago, I preferred to linger
In the shadows at home and read almanacs, calendars and pamphlets

Containing the details of goddess, the origin of migratory planets
The ways the body can be retrieved from the underworld of desire
Defining a particular flower belonging to Erishkigal.
At home, but now I want to travel.

Cassia blossoms define my longing for what is impossible
For nothing that is reasonable, my grandmother, the dowager,
You know the lady from the old country, the weaver of icons,
She's the one that creates all the trouble.

Birds Nesting

Before or after the one had I as many
Years as the crane standing on one foot
Or yet on one another's shores
Reciting the art of divinatory odes

Filling with rain, whatever shoe is left
Fulfills a day of abstinence for pilgrims
Irrespective of their path, whether
Breeding omens in their wake

Or, of their own accord, surrendering,
Drenching invisible footsteps with the wine
Tell no one what you've seen, tell no one what
To do for each shoes worships standing still

Dying

Why refer to death as a casualty and yet
What haunts one curves the breath back into sound
Faltering for an instant, her voice half-lowered,
Grabbing my arm for emphasis, she asks

Maybe it's half-demented you are, my dear
Or maybe blind and deaf, or altogether
Lacking or you are willing trying
To gain a bit of an audience, I suppose

Then I snipped the roses of her compliments
With scissors I used on garden chrysanthemums,
Disheartened by the unsinkable heart of pain
With an air of complacent wisdom, or maybe not

Sipping tea, I retreated to my cave
I huddled in my star quilt that was half-sewn.

Black Hills Gold

Black Hills Gold, a match box, holding the ashes,
Of my husband decidedly made no difference.
From the beginning, whatever had me pegged,
Pegged me entirely in a tented dreams of meadows,

As counterpoints to light, bluebirds, pruning shears.
Shaker chairs, window boxes, gladiolas, lilies,
As well as the hollowed out log canoe
Wherever the stammering river takes us, I flow.

I go with it. I grow with the ghost of love, I weep,
Sister, carrier of the two-fisted pail, mother
Of handkerchiefed aunties, elders, you must enjoy
Scenarios of Euclidian geometry, the pattern:

Tulips, crocus, begonias, semantic idioms
In the aftermath of death in the Yap District
Dive deeply into the planetary mind
The Milky Way surrendering her wine

The Husband

"Let it be known" my neighbor said, "unless you say goodbye
to your husband, once and for all, he will be impressed to visit
you beyond the grave. It's inappropriate. Take the one last
marriage vow, forget him, let him go. Besides, she added, he
never had the nerve to do the gossipy things I did over and
above the call of duty. You never found him, did you, playing
golf at clambake lunches attending astrological conventions or
literary functions? Neither had he the courage to amble through
the breeze way leading to the guarded entrance at Porte de Saint
Cloud on the Avenue de Versailles The scientific community
has failed to represent the exclusiveness of elemental forms off
duty, in this culture. It's not appropriate to erect totem poles in
front of convents.

Sonnet

Undreamt, the riches of a thousand birds,
Who will listen to my secrets now
That I am old and fear the sleeping embers
Of the heart? The ghost that grieves in spring

Is the ghost that weeps in turn for autumn.
Fear sings of a map of famine that sleeping grieves,
A tongueless silence, reckoning up accounts.
Where butterflies swarm over waterfalls, obelisks

Castle walls, pagodas surrender saints
Before painted iconography
An orchard vision is but a surface light
Embroidered in prayer's elusive fire whose inner

And outer flame belies incandescent form.
Therefore, wash the feet of the Siberian groom,
Then drink the transparent water of heirloom.

The Return

I

I let the rabble of goats nibble moss on my roof.
Silence burns the lips of the bearded prophets.
Who has lit a shadows in my tiny room of speech?
A basket of lies holds the pattern, but where I'm walking

Nobody knows the village I am from. There is no floor.
Before it's too late, I sell up everything, and walk to the next village.
Silence takes forever to shape its tattoo on my tongue.
I will not ask what the truth of hunger is while you weep.

If it is not befitting to a ghost that you should weep, than do.
If not, then understand the secret place your life cannot unbend.
If silence shapes your tongue forever mute, so be it.
A thousand thimbles fall like a leafy garment.

II

He who lives out his misery in kindness?
Is that something new, not to be believed?
Whatever I purchased from this city
The money lender has retrieved.
All his birds are placed at a corner of the village.
Who ask nothing of deliverance.

This is the dignity of exile, we all belong to each other.
We hold hostage nothing of the body, only memory,
The memory of speech. I delight in the fact a storm resurrects
The body and slides down the hair of the mountain who sings.

Is nothing yet to be believed?
Know that the Milky Way contains the hive full of souls
Unborn bees have not learned to dance on flowers.

Melon

I thought one way. Now I think another. I eat melon that is
overly ripe. I cook refried beans over a wood stove. Still and all,
Like the next person in the next room, in my life, I feel I am
treading water. Still, I have resisted temptation And have taken
all my clothes to the laundry. I believe in the sanctity of the
Spanish gypsies.

I was a believer. After I wrote this poem, I was also a believer.
How can you tell? Have not all the branches rid themselves of
magnolia flowers? Is my life not seeded by a living god who keeps me
living between lives. Never exceedingly confident in the ambiguity of
the moment, I stick to the speed limit. Who will retrain me not to
think this way? Wasn't Nirvana just around the corner? How can I
forget to live my life? Why must I be so insistent about what I do not
remember?

While observing winged and canny shapes of things to come, what
keeps us from mourning too much? What keeps us from hoping too
much? What keeps us in sympathy with the weather? I dread I will
be kept away from everything I love. It would have been wonderful
if I had had a different life, but I did not. Let me fall back into the
anguish of an ancient flight. I have told you my story. And still like
the ocean, the milkweed plant releases spindrift into clouds. No
doubt, I am still telling the same story and selling insurance. Tell no
one I live in the company of shooting stars.

A portion of the proceeds of this book will be donated
to the education of the children of Zanskar.
for information: www.SaveZanskar.org

CPSIA information can be obtained
at www.ICGtesting.com
Printed in the USA
BVOW03s1732110617

486610BV00001B/20/P